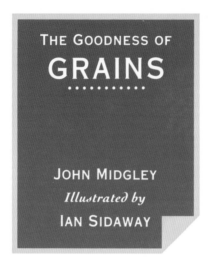

THE GOODNESS OF
GRAINS
· · · · · · · · · ·

JOHN MIDGLEY

Illustrated by

IAN SIDAWAY

RANDOM HOUSE
NEW YORK

ACKNOWLEDGEMENTS
The author thanks Sue Midgley and Jo Swinnerton
for kindly checking the text.

FURTHER READING
Food in History, by Reay Tannahill (Penguin);
For those interested in reading more about food and health
The American Heart Association Cookbook, Fifth Edition
(Random House) and *Superfoods* by Michael Van Straten and
Barbara Griggs (Dorling Kindersley) are recommended.

Published in the United States by Random House, Inc., New York.

This work was published in the United Kingdom by
Pavilion Books Limited, London.

ISBN 0-679-43359-7

Library of Congress Cataloging-in-Publication Data
Midgley, John.
The goodness of grains/John Midgley: illustrated by Ian Sidaway.
p. cm. — (The Goodness of)
ISBN 0-679-43359-7
1. Cookery (Cereals) 2. Cookery (Rice) 3. Grain. I. Title. II. Series:
Midgley, John. Goodness of.
TX808.M53 1994
841.6'31—dc20   93-46528

Manufactured in Hong Kong

2 4 6 8 9 7 5 3

First U.S. Edition

CONTENTS

Part One

Grains *6*

The Goodness of Grains *15*

Grains in History *18*

Part Two

Arroz con Pollo *52*

Banana and Pistachio
Bread *27*

Bulgur Pilaf *62*
Tomato salad
Garlicky yoghurt

Coconut Rice *57*

Corn and Oyster
Mushroom Salad *40*

Couscous and Goat's
Cheese Salad *43*

Couscous with Tagine *64*
Harissa
Couscous and tagine

Cracked Wheat Salad *41*

Focaccia *30*

Fragrant Rice with
Fresh Herbs *56*

Kedgeree *58*
Court bouillon

Muesli Mixture *24*

Mushroom and Pearl
Barley Soup *36*

Nasi Goreng *60*

New England Corn
Chowder *38*

Oat Crunchies *25*

Perfect Polenta *44*

Polenta Pie *46*
Béchamel sauce

Risotto alla Milanese *48*

Rotis *32*

Scotch Broth *34*

Scottish Oatcakes *28*

Tomatoes Stuffed with
Cracked Wheat *42*

Vegetable Risotto *50*

Wild Rice *54*

PART
ONE

. . . .

GRAINS

· · · · · · · · · ·

Grain is defined as 'the seed or corn of a cereal plant'. Named after Ceres, the Roman goddess of agriculture, cereals were developed many thousands of years ago from wild grasses and remain humankind's most important staple foods, many of them vital sources of protein, starch, vitamins and minerals.

Rice, one of the world's largest food crops, is a complete food that is essential to the daily diet of many millions of Asians; over half of the world's population depends on it for survival. Wheat covers more arable land than any other grain. Without wheat, there would be no bread, no pastry, no cakes and biscuits (cookies), and no pasta. Cracked wheat is an important ingredient in the Middle East and parts of central Europe and Asia, while *couscous*, a tiny pasta made from durum wheat, is a staple food in North Africa. Barley, originally cultivated in Mesopotamia by the ancient Sumerians, grows well in many parts of the world. Oats and rye, on the other hand, are invaluable where other cereals do less well, especially in cold climates. Corn is a staple ingredient in the Americas, and millet and sorghum are widely used tropical grains. Buckwheat – also called *kasha* – is not a true grain, but is the fruit of a plant closely related to rhubarb.

Rice

Native to southern China or Indochina, rice *(Oryza sativa)* has been cultivated continuously in wet or flooded land for over 7000 years, and there are as many varieties and hybrids.

Black or white glutinous rice is a short-grained sticky variety that is widely used in China and southeast Asia in both sweet and savoury dishes. Other non-glutinous varieties may be long-, medium- or

short-grained. The Japanese prefer short-grained kinds, which, seasoned with rice vinegar, are a main ingredient in *sushi*, but other Asians use long-grained varieties, such as 'Basmati', from the foothills of the Himalayas, 'Java', and 'Thai fragrant'. In the Middle East and the Balkans, spiced or seasoned rice is a common ingredient in stuffed vegetables, and may be medium- or long-grained. Some parts of Europe are important rice-growing areas, notably the Valencia region of Spain and the Po Valley in Italy, both producing distinguished short- and medium-grained rices which are highly absorbent of cooking liquids; 'Arborio' and 'Valencia' rices are ideal varieties for the superb *risotti* of northern Italy and the wonderful *arrozes* of Spain's Mediterranean coast. The marshy Camargue region of Provence is a small but significant rice-growing area. The United States is one of the leading producers of 'Patna' and 'Carolina' rice, the most common long-grained varieties, which are concentrated in the rice belt of the south-eastern states.

A whole food, brown rice is the unprocessed, husked grain. The cooking time is longer than for 'polished', or white, rice. Pudding rice is a small short-grained variety that is ideal for making rice puddings and other mushy, milky desserts.

A misnomer, 'wild rice' is in fact the seed of *Zizania aquatica*, a North American grass native to Minnesota. Originally gathered in the wild by Indians, this water-loving plant is now widely cultivated. As it takes much longer to cook than true rice, it is usually par-boiled first, then mixed into raw rice and steamed or boiled normally, although it may also be boiled until tender on its own, then combined with nuts, fruit or vegetables and served as an accompaniment to meat, poultry and fish.

Products of rice include Shaohsing wine, rice vinegar and the Japanese spirit *sake*. Rice is also ground into flour, made into noodles and rice 'paper', flaked, and puffed for breakfast cereal.

Wheat

Wheat is native to Egypt and Mesopotamia. The genus divides into *Triticum durum* (hard wheat varieties with a high gluten content) and *Triticum aestivum* (soft low-gluten wheat).

The principal wheat products are: flour; semolina; wheat berries (the whole grain with only the husk removed); cracked wheat (split wheat berries); a partly cooked form of cracked wheat called *bulgur, burghul* or *bulgar;* rolled wheat; flaked wheat; sprouted wheat; wheat germ; and wheat bran.

Most of the world's wheat is milled into flour. To make white flour, wheat berries are ground by metal or stone rollers, then sieved to remove the unwanted germ and bran. The flour can then be bleached to make a white flour or left unbleached for a creamier-coloured flour. White flour is treated with iron, thiamine and riboflavin, which are all present in the wheat germ and bran. Most plain (all-purpose) flour is a blend of hard and soft wheat. Self-raising (self-rising) flour has baking powder added. Wholemeal (whole wheat) flour retains some or all of the wheat-germ and bran; the best is ground by millstones and sold as 'stone-ground' flour. 'Granary' flour is wholemeal flour with 'kibbled', or cracked, wheat added.

Semolina should not be confused with semolina flour, which is a flour milled from the endosperm, or heart, of durum wheat that is mainly used by pasta manufacturers. Semolina is a granular product of durum wheat which varies in texture from medium-fine to coarse, and which is used chiefly in milk puddings, *gnocchi* and as a thickening agent. It is also sprinkled on layers of fresh egg pasta to prevent them from sticking together.

Whole wheat berries may be cooked like rice or they may be sprouted and added to salads. Cracked wheat, particularly *bulgur,* is a very popular and versatile grain throughout the Middle East. Soaking in water swells the grains or they may be simmered until soft and used in salads, pilafs and stuffings, but *bulgur* is best known as the main ingredient in Lebanese *tabbouleh. Couscous* may be prepared in much the same way as *bulgur.* Together with a fiery spice mixture called *harissa, couscous* is the traditional accompaniment to rich North African stews, or *tagines.* Most of the *couscous* that is sold has been precooked and only needs soaking in water to swell the grains, and heating. Rolled wheat, flaked wheat, wheat germ and wheat bran are widely used in baking and added to breakfast cereal.

Barley

Barley *(Hordeum vulgare)* is used mainly by brewers of beer and malt vinegar and by Scotch whisky distillers. The barley must first be malted and the grain allowed to ferment before being dried and ground.

For culinary purposes, barley is sold hulled, hulled and stripped ('Scotch' or 'pot barley') or hulled and polished ('pearl barley'). The first two forms are slow to cook, while pearl barley, which is usually added to soups, becomes swollen and tender in half the time. Malted barley is also added to milkshakes and may be used in baking.

Oats and rye

These grains are an invaluable source of flour and meal in harsh cold climates or where other cold-tolerant cereals, such as wheat and barley, cannot be grown successfully.

Oats *(Avena sativa)* are native to Europe and are

an old Scottish staple food. Commonly available in several different forms, husked oats left whole are called groats; they are also ground into oatmeal, which is used to make Scottish oatcakes; they can be rolled and added to breakfast cereals and muesli; or they can be rolled and flaked to make porridge. Also available are 'jumbo' oats, crushed oats and oat flour.

Rye flour is milled from the whole grains of *Secale cereale* and features in the dark sourdough breads of Russia and other northern European countries, usually blended with wheat flour. In Scandinavia, it is also used to bake biscuits and crispbreads. Like barley, rye is converted into whisky, especially in Canada.

Corn

Native to the Americas, where it has been grown for thousands of years, corn (*Zea mais*) divides into two groups: sweetcorn and field corn.

There are over 200 varieties of sweetcorn, which may be white, yellow or multi-coloured. Sweetcorn is treated as a vegetable and is very versatile. Corn cobs can be boiled or grilled (broiled) whole, or the kernels can be removed. Sweetcorn kernels can be cooked in soups and stews; added to salads; served alone or added to mixed vegetables to accompany meat and poultry; puréed and made into fritters; or pickled and turned into relishes. Whole baby cobs are increasingly fashionable and are particularly delicious stir-fried. The dried kernels of certain varieties puff up when fried in oil, making popcorn. Sweetcorn also produces syrup and flour for breads and chips, and blue corn makes a greyish cornmeal.

With a higher starch content, field corn is milled to produce cornmeal and corn-flour. It is also pressed for oil, and made into hominy and hominy grits. In the United States, boiled cornmeal is called cornmeal

13

mush; Italians call it *polenta* and Romanians know it as *mamaliga*. The mush may also be allowed to solidify, then sliced and fried, baked or grilled. American cornflour is mixed with bicarbonate of soda (baking soda) and turned into wonderful corn breads. In Mexico, more finely milled cornflour is used to make many different flatbreads such as *tortillas, tacos, tostadas* and corn chips.

When corn is grown as a staple food great care must be taken to supplement it with foods rich in vitamin C. By contrast, people can subsist for quite long periods on a diet of brown rice, wholemeal (whole wheat) bread or potatoes, which are much closer to complete foods.

Millet and sorghum

Millet (*Panicum miliaceum*) and sorghum (*Sorghum vulgare*) are closely related. Although millet was once widely grown in Europe and does well in temperate climates, now, as in Neolithic times, it is mainly grown in hot regions, especially Africa and India. It can be cooked like rice and makes a good flour. Sorghum also grows well in tropical countries, where it is a staple cereal, but is also cultivated for its sweet sap, which is converted into syrup and sugar.

Cereals are the best source of complex carbohydrates, which are essential to health. Doctors and nutritionists are urging us to increase our intake of starchy foods, especially whole grains. Moreover, evidence increasingly suggests that starch provides even better protection against cancers of the intestine and colon than plant fibre.

Grains also have a high vitamin, mineral and protein content. When paired with beans, peas and lentils, grains offer the best balance of essential amino acids and a particularly rich supply of protein.

Recent studies point to the beneficial role of antioxidants, such as vitamins B, C and E, and minerals, such as selenium. Antioxidants keep the body generally healthy and supple, and delay ageing. More specifically, they protect against cancers and heart disease by neutralizing unstable and potentially damaging molecules called 'free radicals'. Whole grains are a good source of antioxidants.

Grains appear to be beneficial in other ways too.

A rice diet, for example, helps to reduce high blood pressure. In traditional medicine, rice is also prescribed to treat intestinal and urinary-tract disorders, and can help to dissolve kidney stones. Boiled rice and its cooking water are offered to diarrhoea sufferers. Rice is believed to regulate blood sugar levels and is therefore sometimes recommended to diabetics. Unpolished or brown rice is especially rich in vitamins and fibre.

Like unpolished rice, millet is highly nutritious and rich in protein, but has less starch. Millet is an excellent source of silicon and is therefore especially good for the health of our hair, skin, eyes, nails and teeth.

Barley water has long been prescribed to invalids and convalescents as a tonic. Barley contains many vitamins and minerals and can help to reduce blood cholesterol. Like rice, barley can soothe inflammations of the intestinal and urinary tracts.

Oats were once a staple food in the Scottish highlands and provide plenty of protein, B-complex vitamins, vitamin E, calcium, potassium and magnesium. Traditionally used by herbalists to treat a wide variety of conditions, oats are now recognized as an extraordinarily effective health food that can reduce high blood cholesterol and help to prevent cardiovascular disease and cancer.

Corn, though nutritious, must be supplemented by vitamin C. For the corn-growing Aztecs and Incas, native tomatoes, potatoes and chilies provided a rich source of vitamin C. Butter and cheese, the traditional accompaniments to the Italian *polenta* (cornmeal mush), are equally good sources. Acute dairy shortages in northern Italy have led to periodic outbreaks of pellagra, an endemic disease often ending in insanity caused by vitamin deficiency. Pellagra was once frequent among the peasants of Lombardy and still ravages many African communities today.

GRAINS IN HISTORY
· · · · · · · · · ·

Grains have played a pre-eminent role in history ever since they were first gathered in the wild. Barley, millet and wheat were the first crops grown in Mesopotamia and Egypt, probably as early 7000BC, and certainly around 5000BC, by which time irrigation was in place. Rye was a weed of the wheat fields. Rice was first cultivated in southern China or Indochina some 7000 years ago, and wild corn was gathered in Mexico at around the same time. Pasta has existed at least since ancient Greece, but pasta of one kind or another was also eaten by a host of civilizations: the Etruscans, Chinese, Tibetans, Mongolians, Afghans, Indians and Persians.

Wild grain motivated Neolithic hunter-gatherers to form permanent settlements. As Reay Tannahill explains in *Food in History*, mature wild cereal plants burst open to release their edible grain, and agricultural settlements probably evolved from opportunistic encampments pitched near the ripening grain for quick and easy access to food.

By 2500BC, precise written instructions for the efficient planting of barley seed had been recorded in a Sumerian farmers' almanac. Nearly half of the barley crop was fermented to make ale, which was also brewed from wheat. Brewing appears to have been discovered accidentally as a by-product of baking.

The Egyptians were also great brewers and prolific ale-drinkers, and are credited with the discovery of leavened bread, whether by accidental contamination of dough with wild yeasts or by a deliberate substitution of ale for water in the dough mix. The Greeks traded with the Egyptians, importing their grain. From the earliest times, the Greek diet revolved around grains, especially barley gruel and breads made from wheat, millet and barley flour.

The Roman policy of granting grain subsidies, at

times even distributing free grain to the citizens of Rome created a massive demand for wheat, which was imported from Egypt, Sicily and North Africa. The political control of wheat-producing countries as far afield as Britain gave a vital impetus to Roman hegemony, and a demand for better distribution of the grain led to great improvements and innovations in shipping. To wealthy Romans, many different breads were available, some, much like the fashionable breads of today, flavoured with honey, oil or cheese, and others that were flat and crisp and intended for dipping in wine. The poor, however, subsisted on coarse bread and *pulmentum,* a millet porridge which the Romans acquired from the Etruscans, and which was later made from ground chestnuts until the discovery and planting of American corn created the modern version, *polenta.*

During the Dark Ages, bread continued to provide vital sustenance and was the European staple food, supplemented by whatever scraps of meat and vegetables could be added to the ubiquitous, constantly simmering soup cauldron. Together with bread, a spiced and sweetened wheat porridge called *frumenty* provided nourishment, especially during Lent.

In much of Europe, bread was baked daily with a combination of rye and wheat flour, since rye grew amidst the wheat and was very tolerant of cold. Occasionally, however, a severe penalty had to be paid for rye dependence: ergotism. First afflicting Germany in AD857, outbreaks of ergotism were always calamitous. All cereals are susceptible to fungal smuts and rusts, but the fungus *Claviceps purpurea* (rye ergot) can contaminate rye so severely that even the intense heat of the bread oven cannot destroy its cocktail of toxins. (One such toxin is lysergic acid diethylamide – LSD.) These induce in the hapless victim a host of terrible symptoms, ranging from potentially gangrenous skin inflammations to dementia and death. The condition's vernacular names of 'holy fire ' and 'St. Anthony's fire' referred to the victims' hot, red skin, the acceptance of the affliction as divine retribution, and to the belief that St. Anthony could intercede on behalf of supplicants. Other destructive rusts periodically decimated wheat crops, causing great famines.

In India, rice, millet and wheat are all ancient staple foods, rice occurring where the land was well watered or liable to frequent flooding. Boiled rice and millet, millet batters, and flat wheat breads, being bland and absorbent of sauces, have long provided an excellent base for the many traditional meat, vegetable, dried bean and lentil curries of the subcontinent.

In China, just as in Egypt and Mesopotamia, grains such as rice and millet have been used for both food and alcoholic drinks. Rice and millet were made into wine but were also acetified for vinegar, which has been an invaluable condiment in the sophisticated cuisines of China, Korea and Japan. For thousands of years, flour has been milled from rice, wheat and millet. Wheat and rice noodles were popular throughout the region by AD100. By the Middle Ages, China had acquired hundreds of different rice varieties, each one valued for its own unique fragrance and flavour.

The Persians adopted the rice of the Indians and developed an extraordinary repertoire of exquisite rice dishes, showing a flair equal to that of the Chinese. The Arabs, long familiar with barley, millet and wheat, discovered rice during their Persian conquest and introduced it into Spain. Rice and all manner of grains besides remain popular in many different forms throughout the region.

The race to dominate the spice trade in the fifteenth century produced unforeseen and far-reaching consequences. When Columbus landed in the Caribbean islands – mistaking them for the Indies, home of pepper – he stumbled across corn, which the *Taino* Indians called *mahiz*; hence the English word 'maize'. (In the Andes, wherever the land was too high and too cold to grow corn, the Spaniards found potatoes instead.) American Indians had already developed hundreds of varieties of corn by the time of the Discovery, and the Aztecs of Mexico used corn for their daily porridge and to make flatbreads, to which were added chili peppers, avocados, beans and tomatoes. The Spaniards took corn to the Philippines, whence it soon reached China, but the Portuguese were responsible for introducing corn into Africa. In North America, durable, portable supplies of cornmeal and dried corn sustained the early settlers in their journeys westwards.

By the turn of the century, improvements in agricultural technology, especially in ploughing, harvesting and threshing, and the development of the American railroad system permitted the mass production of grain in the vast arable spaces of the midwest, creating cheap exportable grain that permanently altered the pattern of agriculture in much of Europe. Russia also developed her extensive granaries soon afterwards, and before long, European wheat production dwindled, to be replaced by other, more specialized produce, such as bacon, dairy goods, fruit and vegetables. With the advance of food technology, grains have become more and more refined, with much of their goodness removed. This current decade has seen a strong reaction against that trend, and people are demanding a return to more traditional whole foods.

The following recipes have been culled from several different culinary traditions from countries where grains are highly esteemed.

RICE

PART
TWO

· · · · · · · · · ·

BULGHUR
WHEAT

MUESLI MIXTURE

Dried fruits give this muesli mixture ample sweetness so sugar is unnecessary. Just add a little milk to enjoy this nourishing breakfast. This recipe makes about 675g/1½lb of muesli, which should keep well for several weeks.

400g/14oz/4 cups regular oats
110g/4oz/1½ cups plain or malted wheat flakes
110g/4oz raisins
110g/4oz dried figs, chopped
110g/4oz dried dates, chopped
110g/4oz chopped Brazil nuts
50g/2oz dried banana slices, broken into small pieces
50g/2oz sunflower seeds
50g/2oz pumpkin seeds

Put all the ingredients into a large mixing bowl and mix thoroughly. Keep in an air-tight container and store in a cool, dark place.

OAT CRUNCHIES
· · · · · · · · · ·

This makes about 575g/1/¹⁄₄ lb of delicious, crunchy oat biscuits (cookies). Called 'flapjacks' in Britain, they are not to be confused with American flapjacks (which are pancakes). This traditional recipe was kindly provided by a friend who has been making them since childhood. They are the ideal tea-time snack, and especially popular with children.

110g/4oz/¹⁄₄ cup butter
2 tbs golden syrup
110g/4oz/1 cup self-raising (self-rising) flour
225g/8oz/1 cup caster (superfine) sugar
225g/8oz/1³⁄₄ cups porridge oats

Place the butter and syrup in a small pan and heat gently until the butter has melted.

Preheat the oven to 190°C/375°F/gas mark 5. Sift the flour into a large bowl, add the sugar and oats and mix thoroughly. Stir in the butter and syrup; when thoroughly combined turn the mixture into a shallow baking tin, press down firmly to make an even, flat surface and bake for 15 minutes. Remove from the oven, score into squares and serve when cooled. The oat crunchies will keep well in an airtight container.

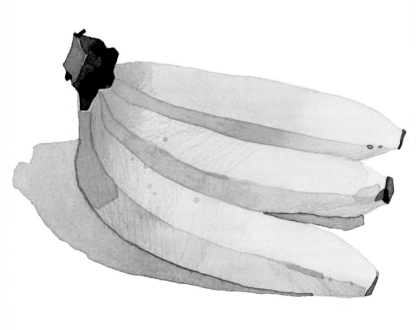

BANANA AND PISTACHIO BREAD

This delicious sweet bread is closer in style and tex-ture to a cake and is the perfect accompaniment to afternoon tea. The pistachios give an attractive green colour, while the cooked banana creates a dark, flecked appearance and a wonderful aroma, which is irre-sistible to adults and children alike. This makes 2 loaves, each one weighing about 450g/1lb.

3 ripe bananas
110g/4oz/$\frac{1}{4}$ cup butter
225g/8oz/1 cup vanilla sugar
(or 225g/8oz/1 cup caster (superfine) sugar and 1 tsp vanilla essence)
2 eggs
275g/10oz/$2\frac{1}{4}$ cups plain (all-purpose) flour
1 tsp bicarbonate of soda (baking soda)
1 tsp salt
75g/3oz shelled pistachio nuts, chopped

Mash the bananas. Pre-heat the oven to 180°C/ 375°F/gas mark 5.

Cream together the butter and sugar; when pale, beat in the eggs. Sift the flour into the mixture and add the bicarbonate of soda, salt, mashed bananas and chopped pistachio nuts. Mix thoroughly, spoon into 2 loaf tins and bake for 45 minutes or until the loaves are golden brown. Cool on a wire rack. (May be frozen.)

Scottish Oatcakes

Oatcakes are hard biscuits (cookies) which Scots eat with butter, cheese, jams – even herrings. They are simple to make and store well. This makes about 20 circular oatcakes, each about 10cm/4 inches in diameter.

575g/1¼lb/5 cups oatmeal
1½ tsp salt
25g/1oz/2 tbs butter, at room temperature
225ml/8fl oz/1 cup water

Pre-heat the oven to 200°C/400°F/gas mark 6.

Put about 450g/1lb/4 cups of the oatmeal into a bowl. Add the salt and rub in the butter with your fingers. Add the water and mix well with a spoon. Apply more oatmeal to a clean work surface. Dust your hands with oatmeal and knead the dough for about 2 minutes. Apply a little more oatmeal to the surface of the dough, then roll it out as thinly as possible, adding a little more oatmeal to prevent the dough from sticking. Stamp out about 20 rounds with the rim of a coffee cup. Place the oatcakes on a baking tray and bake for 12 minutes. Turn them over and bake for 5 minutes longer. Cool on a rack and store in an airtight container.

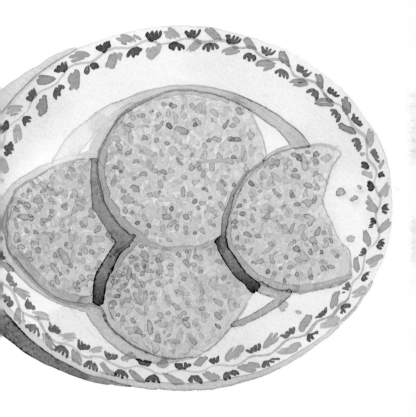

FOCACCIA
. . . .

Made with olive oil, seasoned with sea salt and flavoured with rosemary or sage, focaccia is a delicious flat bread from Italy. As a variation, substitute for the herbs finely chopped fried pancetta or bacon, sausage meat, sliced onion, or grilled (broiled) vegetables. Baked in a large rectangular tin (pan) or in a round oven dish, the focaccia is sliced and can be devoured alone as a snack or eaten with Parma ham, sun-dried tomatoes, cheeses and pickles. This version makes enough for four people.

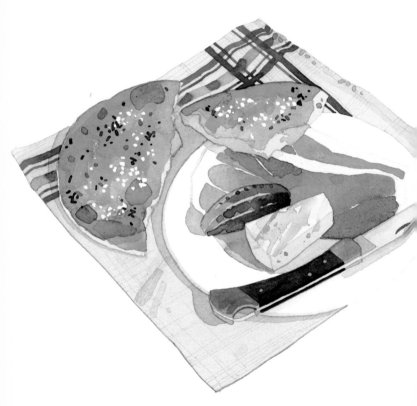

400g/14oz/3$\frac{1}{2}$ cups strong plain (all-purpose) flour
3 tsp sea salt
1$\frac{1}{2}$ tsp easy dried yeast (about half a packet)
110ml/4fl oz/$\frac{1}{2}$ cup extra virgin olive oil
225ml/8fl oz/1 cup warm water
leaves from 2 sprigs of sage, finely chopped
leaves from 2 sprigs of rosemary, finely chopped

Mix the flour, 1 tsp salt, yeast and 2 tbs of oil in a bowl. Add the water gradually, kneading all the while by hand or with a machine fitted with dough hooks. When the dough is smooth (after 15 minutes of kneading by hand or 5 minutes of machine-kneading), lift it out with floured hands and transfer to an oiled container. Cover with a clean cloth and leave to rest somewhere warm until it has doubled in size (1–2 hours).

Dust your hands, a work surface and a rolling pin with flour. Pre-heat the oven to 220°C/425°F/gas mark 7. Knock back the risen dough and knead by hand for 1 minute. Oil some large, wide and shallow oven-proof containers; this recipe makes sufficient dough to fit snugly into two 28 × 18cm/11 × 7inch oven trays or two 25cm/10inch circular oven pans. Roll out the dough (not too thinly) and fit it into the containers, stretching so that the dough touches all the edges. Make regular indentations on the dough surface with the ball of your thumb. Pour over the remaining oil and spread it over the entire surface. Sprinkle with the remaining salt, scatter over the herbs and bake for 15 minutes or until golden. Divide into generous sections. *Focaccia* is best enjoyed hot but may be served at any temperature.

ROTIS

· · · · · · · · · ·

Rotis and *chapatis* are the everyday unleavened bread of northern India and Pakistan and accompany almost every meal. A special kind of wheat flour called *ata*, which is also labelled 'chapati flour', can be bought in Asian grocery stores and supermarkets, but a mixture of wholemeal and plain (all-purpose) flour may be substituted. The dough discs are cooked 'dry', one at a time, on a wide cast iron griddle, pre-heated until very hot; a wide, shallow, heavy-bottomed pan also produces excellent results. Makes 10–12 *rotis*.

275g/10oz/2¼ cups chapati flour
(or 110g/4oz/1 cup sieved wholemeal flour and
175g/6oz/1¼ cups plain flour)
1 tbs oil
170ml/6fl oz/³⁄₄ cup water

Mix the flour with the oil and a little water; kneading by hand or with a machine fitted with dough hooks, add the rest of the water. Knead until the dough is soft, smooth and elastic (about 10 minutes' hand-kneading, less by machine). With floured hands, lift out the dough and put it into a lightly oiled container, cover with a cloth and rest for 30 minutes.

With floured hands, divide the dough into 10–12 balls of equal size, adding a little extra flour to prevent the dough from sticking. Flatten each one against the palm of one hand, press onto a floured work surface and, with a floured rolling pin, roll out 10–12 discs, each 15cm/6 inches in diameter. Preheat the griddle or pan for several minutes. When very hot, place a *roti* on the surface. After 30 seconds, turn to cook the other side. The *roti* should be dry and speckled with brown spots. Remove and serve immediately or wrap in foil to keep warm (each cooked *roti* may be buttered). Repeat until all the *rotis* are cooked. Suitable for freezing.

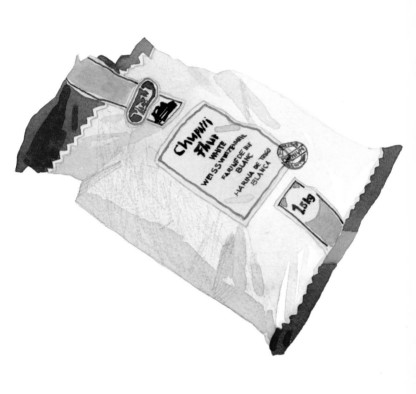

SCOTCH BROTH

. . . .

Scotch broth (barley broth) can be made with what-ever vegetables are available: leeks, carrots and onions are the most common, and cabbage and pota-toes may be added. The essential ingredients are the lamb, the pearl barley and the leeks. This version makes enough for six people.

handful of fresh parsley, including stalks, washed
450g/1lb lean lamb
110g/4oz/$\frac{1}{2}$ cup pearl barley
2 litres/3$\frac{1}{2}$ pints/7 cups water
225g/8oz carrots, scrubbed and chopped
450g/1lb leeks, chopped
1 large onion, peeled and chopped
2 sticks (stalks) of celery, washed and chopped
2 bay leaves
salt
freshly milled black pepper

Put to one side two whole sprigs of parsley; detach the leaves from the rest of the parsley and chop them finely, retaining the stalks. Remove and discard all visible fat from the lamb and shred the meat.

Put the lamb, pearl barley and water into a pot. Cover and bring to the boil, then reduce the heat and simmer with a cover on for 45 minutes, removing and discarding any scum. Add the vegetables, bay leaves, whole sprigs of parsley, parsley stalks, and season. Cover again and simmer for 1 hour. Check the seasoning, remove the parsley stalks, sprinkle with the reserved chopped parsley and serve with wholemeal bread.

MUSHROOM AND PEARL BARLEY SOUP

This very traditional Polish soup is packed full of flavour and nourishment, and makes an agreeably filling lunch or supper for four people.

16g/²/₃oz dried porcini mushrooms
4 tbs sunflower oil
25g/1oz/2 tbs butter
1 shallot, peeled and finely chopped
175g/6oz mushrooms, wiped clean and finely chopped
salt
freshly milled black pepper
generous handful of fresh parsley, washed and chopped
1 onion, peeled and chopped
small carrot, scrubbed and diced
1½ litres/2¾ pints/5½ cups chicken stock (broth)
110g/4oz/½ cup pearl barley

Soak the dried mushrooms in a cup of hot water for about 20 minutes, then remove and chop them. Strain and reserve their soaking liquid.

Heat half the oil and all the butter in a frying pan. Add the shallots and let them colour slightly, then add the mushrooms and season. Sauté until they have reduced to a dense, dryish consistency. (This will take about 20 minutes – a little longer if the mushrooms exude a lot of moisture). Stir in half the parsley, then set aside the cooked mushroom mixture.

Heat the remaining oil in a soup pan. Fry the onion and carrot until lightly coloured. Stir in the chopped reconstituted porcini and the cooked mushroom mixture. Pour in the stock and the porcini's soaking liquid. Add the pearl barley. Season and bring to the boil. Reduce the heat to minimum, cover, and simmer for about 1½ hours. Stir in the remaining parsley, check the seasoning and serve accompanied by a stack of buttered slices of rye bread.

NEW ENGLAND CORN CHOWDER

· · · · · · · · · ·

This nourishing soup can be made with canned or frozen corn. However, the best time to make corn chowder is from August to October, when fresh corn on the cob is so good and plentiful. Chowder is named after a *chaudière*, the traditional French pot for soup-making. This serves six.

4 corn cobs, husked
(or 400g/14oz canned or frozen corn kernels, thawed)
840ml/1 ½ pints/3 cups water
1 medium onion, peeled and halved from top to bottom
3 tbs olive oil
75g/3oz lean bacon, trimmed and diced
350g/12oz potatoes, peeled and diced
2 bay leaves
sprig of sage
salt
freshly milled black pepper
560ml/1 pint/2 cups milk

Boil the corn cobs in salted water until just tender (10–12 minutes), then drain. When cool, hold the corn cobs upright and sever the kernels with a sharp knife, cutting down from end to end. Reserve approximately one quarter of the kernels. Put the rest into a food processor with 225ml/8fl oz/1 cup of water. Process to a purée and set aside. Meanwhile, slice each onion half thinly and set aside.

Heat the oil in a soup pan. Fry the bacon until just crisp, then remove and set it aside. Fry the onion until lightly coloured, add the potatoes and stir-fry for 2–3 minutes. Add the corn purée, the bacon, remaining water, and herbs. Season generously. Bring to the boil, cover and simmer for 25 minutes. By now the potatoes should have dissolved into the soup; if not, squash them against the sides of the pot with the back of a spoon and mix thoroughly. Add the reserved corn kernels and cook for about 5 minutes longer. Add the milk and heat through. Check the seasoning and serve very hot.

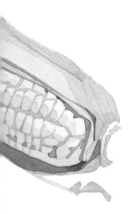

Corn and Oyster Mushroom Salad

Pretty shell-pink, chromium-yellow and dove-grey oyster mushrooms are cultivated by growers of 'exotic' mushrooms and may be found in larger super-markets and specialist food stores. When combined with fresh corn, thinly sliced oyster mushrooms make an unusual but delicious salad. If you cannot find any oyster mushrooms, very fresh button mushrooms may be substituted. This serves four, accompanied by slices of wholemeal bread.

3 cobs of corn, husked
3 tbs extra virgin olive oil
1 tbs wine or sherry vinegar
salt
freshly milled black pepper
175g/6oz oyster mushrooms, sliced
(leave very small ones whole)
generous handful of fresh parsley, washed and chopped

Boil the corn in salted water until tender (12–15 minutes). When cool enough to touch, cut the kernels from the cobs with a sharp knife. Transfer them to a salad bowl and break up any clusters. Beat the olive oil with the vinegar, salt and pepper. Mix in the remaining ingredients, pour the dressing over them and mix well. Serve immediately.

CRACKED WHEAT SALAD
· · · · · · · · · · ·

This is my version of a Lebanese dish called *tabbouleh*. It differs from more traditional recipes in that the *bulgur* (cracked wheat) is first simmered until soft, then combined with shredded salad vegetables and chopped olives in addition to the mandatory parsley, mint, olive oil and lemon juice. Makes enough for six people.

225g/8oz/1½ cups *bulgur*
560ml/1 pint/2 cups water
juice of 1 lemon
140ml/5fl oz/²⁄₃ cup olive oil
small bunch of fresh parsley, washed and finely chopped
small bunch of mint, washed and finely chopped
225g/8oz tomatoes, washed and finely chopped
110g/4oz lettuce, washed, shaken dry and finely chopped
4 spring onions (scallions), washed and thinly sliced
12 stoned (pitted) black olives, finely chopped
salt
freshly milled black pepper

Put the *bulgur* into a pan with the water. Bring to the boil, cover, reduce the heat and simmer for 15 minutes; the water should all be absorbed and the *bulgur* tender. Allow to cool.

Combine all the ingredients, season well and mix again. Let stand for 30–60 minutes to allow the flavours to develop, and serve with warm *pita* bread.

TOMATOES STUFFED WITH CRACKED WHEAT

· · · · · · · · · ·

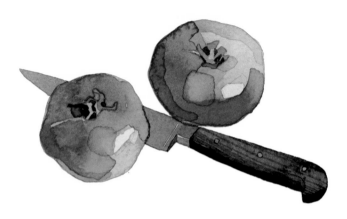

Tabbouleh (see the recipe for cracked wheat salad) makes an excellent vegetarian stuffing for large tomatoes and other vegetables. You can use up any left-over salad or make the original cracked wheat salad recipe: 225g/8oz is sufficient to stuff four large tomatoes. Serves four as an appetizer, two as a light lunch or supper dish.

4 beefsteak or marmande tomatoes
225g/8oz cracked wheat salad
salt
freshly milled black pepper
225ml/8fl oz/1 cup vegetable stock (broth)

Pre-heat the oven to 180°C/350°F/gas mark 4.

Slice off and discard the tomatoes' caps. Carefully scoop out the cavities, retaining thick walls with a good layer of flesh. Fill with cracked wheat salad and stand the tomatoes upright in a shallow oven-proof container. Season, pour the stock over them and bake until tender but not too soft (about 20 minutes). Serve hot.

COUSCOUS AND GOAT'S CHEESE SALAD

. . . .

Like cracked wheat, *couscous* swells when soaked in water and the soft grains make a very good salad base, to which can be added fresh herbs and melted fried goat's cheese. Serves four people as an appetizer.

200g/7oz/1 cup *couscous*
water
salt
freshly milled black pepper
$\frac{1}{2}$ tsp cayenne
6 tbs extra virgin olive oil
juice of 1 lemon
handful of fresh mint, washed and chopped
handful of fresh parsley, washed and chopped
small bunch of fresh chives, washed and snipped
4 firm tomatoes, peeled and chopped
12 stoned (pitted) black olives, chopped
225g/8oz goat's cheese, rinded and cubed
flour
olive oil

Put the *couscous* into a bowl and pour in just enough water to give a thin covering. Leave until the grains have swollen and the water has been absorbed. Stir with your fingers to break up any lumps. Put the *couscous* into a salad bowl. Season generously with salt, pepper and cayenne. Beat the extra virgin olive oil with the lemon juice. Add the fresh herbs, tomatoes and olives to the salad, pour over the oil and lemon juice dressing and mix thoroughly. Cover the bowl and refrigerate for at least 2 hours.

Roll the cheese in flour. Heat a shallow layer of oil in a non-stick frying pan. Fry the cheese very briefly; it will quickly begin to melt. Drain and dot soft lumps of cheese over the *couscous*. Serve straight away.

PERFECT POLENTA

· · · · · · · · · · ·

The following recipe for *polenta* (yellow cornmeal) is practically foolproof. Although traditionally the polenta is enriched with plenty of butter, the substitution of a little olive oil makes a very tasty and healthier *polenta*. Eaten while still hot, soft and steaming, it's the perfect cold-weather accompaniment to all manner of rustic stews and sauces. In northern Italy, where it is a staple food, it is often paired with wild mushrooms braised with wine or tomatoes. Alternatively, it can be poured on to a wooden board while still hot, levelled with the back of a wooden spoon to make an even layer about 2cm/³⁄₄ inch thick, then allowed to cool and solidify. This *polenta* 'cake' can then be sliced into uniform sections and fried in olive oil, grilled (broiled) or baked.

1¹⁄₂ litres/2¹⁄₂ pints/5¹⁄₂ cups water
375g/13oz/2 generous cups Italian 'instant' *polenta*
(sometimes labelled 5 minuti)
4 tbs olive oil
50g/2oz/¹⁄₄ cup freshly grated parmesan cheese
freshly milled black pepper

Bring the water to a boil in a capacious pot, adding about 2 tsp salt. Rain in the *polenta* with one hand, while you stir all the while with the other. Keep stirring while the *polenta* thickens and sputters like molten lava; it will come cleanly away from the sides of the pot after 5 minutes or so. Stir in the remaining ingredients while still piping hot and mix thoroughly.

POLENTA PIE
....

Cooked *polenta* that has been allowed to solidify forms the basis of many delicious pies and *timbales* in northern Italy. Here is my own very tasty *polenta* pie, made with *polenta* from the preceding recipe, which serves four people.

375g/13oz/2 generous cups Italian 'instant' *polenta*,
cooked, solidified and sliced
(see introduction to previous recipe)
225ml/8fl oz/1 cup béchamel sauce (see recipe opposite)
110ml/4fl oz/¹/₂ cup tomato *passata* (crushed tomatoes)
1 clove of garlic, peeled and finely chopped
handful of fresh basil leaves, washed and torn into pieces
salt
freshly milled black pepper
150g/5oz/generous ¹/₂ cup Italian mozzarella cheese,
chopped
50g/2oz/¹/₄ cup freshly grated parmesan cheese
olive oil

Pre-heat the oven to 200°C/400°F/gas mark 6. Lightly oil an oblong oven pan large enough to accommodate all the *polenta* in one layer.

Fit the *polenta* to the pan base, cutting if necessary to fill any gaps. Spread the béchamel sauce evenly over the *polenta*, spoon the tomato over that, then sprinkle with garlic and scatter with the basil. Season, then dot with mozzarella. Sprinkle the parmesan over the pie and finish with a dribble of olive oil.

Bake for 25–30 minutes or until a golden crust has formed. Serve hot, accompanied by a salad.

Béchamel sauce
1 onion, peeled and quartered
2 cloves
1 bay leaf
salt
freshly milled black pepper
560ml/1 pint/2 cups milk
25g/1oz/2 tbs butter
25g/1oz/3 tbs flour

Put the onion, cloves, bay leaf, seasoning and milk into a pan. Bring to the boil, turn off the heat and set aside for 10 minutes. Strain the milk.

Melt the butter in another pan. Stir in the flour and cook over a low heat for 2–3 minutes. Add the milk very gradually while whisking continuously over a low heat until the sauce is very smooth and creamy. Check the seasoning. May be used immediately or cover and refrigerate for up to 3–4 days; remove the skin and mix well before using.

RISOTTO ALLA MILANESE

Thiselegant risotto is surprisingly easy to make, but try to use genuine *arborio* rice, real saffron strands (not the powdered variety) and authentic parmesan cheese. This makes a sublime first course, although traditionally the risotto accompanies the Milanese speciality, *ossobucco* (braised shin of veal). Serves four.

1 litre/1¾ pints/3½ cups chicken stock (broth)
½ tsp saffron strands
140ml/5fl oz/½ cup hot milk
50g/2oz/4 tbs butter
2 tbs olive oil
50g/2oz finely chopped bacon
1 small onion, peeled and finely chopped
300g/11oz/1¼ cups *arborio* rice
salt
freshly milled black pepper
50g/2oz/¼ cup parmesan, freshly grated

Bring the stock to simmering point in a covered pan. Set aside. Put the saffron in a cup. Pour in the hot milk and set aside.

Heat half of the butter and all the olive oil in a wide, heavy, well-seasoned frying pan. When the butter has melted but before it burns, add the bacon and onion. Sauté until the onion is soft and lightly coloured and the bacon is just crisp, stirring constantly. Add the rice and stir-fry over a medium heat for 2–3 minutes. Season. Add some of the hot stock and stir continuously until the rice has absorbed the liquid. Continue adding more stock in stages until it has all been used up and the rice is tender but no longer soupy – this will take about 25 minutes. Pour in the saffron liquid after about 15 minutes' cooking.

Mix in the remaining butter and half the cheese; serve the remaining cheese in a separate bowl.

VEGETABLE RISOTTO

· · · · · · · · · ·

This nourishing and very tasty vegetarian risotto can be made with all kinds of fresh vegetables not just the ones listed below. Any leftovers can be shaped into golf balls or sausages, rolled in flour and fried until golden; serve with mayonnaise. This makes enough for four people.

1 litre/1¾ pints/3½ cups vegetable stock (broth)
25g/1oz/2 tbs butter
4 tbs olive oil
1 onion, peeled and chopped
1 stick (stalk) of celery, thinly sliced
2 cloves of garlic, peeled and chopped
110g/4oz cauliflower or broccoli, washed and chopped
110g/4oz green beans, washed and chopped
110g/4oz garden sorrel or spinach, washed and shredded
110g/4oz mushrooms, sliced
350g/12oz ripe tomatoes, washed, peeled and chopped
salt
freshly milled black pepper
300g/11oz/1¼ cups *arborio* rice
75g/3oz/⅓ cup parmesan cheese, freshly grated

Heat the vegetable stock in a covered pan and put it on one side as soon as it simmers. Heat the butter and oil in a wide, heavy frying pan. Add the onion and celery and sauté until soft and lightly coloured. Add the garlic, mix and sauté for 1 minute. Add all the remaining vegetables except the tomatoes, and stir-fry for 6–8 minutes. Add the tomatoes, mix well and cook for 5–6 minutes longer. Season, add the rice and sauté with the vegetables for 2 minutes.

Re-heat the stock and proceed as in the preceding recipe, adding a little water if the stock is exhausted. Mix in half of the parmesan and serve the remaining cheese separately in a bowl.

Arroz con Pollo

This rudimentary *paella* is rarely to be found in restaurants, but belongs instead to simple Spanish home-cooking. It contains no seafood, only rice, chicken and its stock (broth), saffron and vegetables. (The name of the dish means quite simply 'rice with chicken'.) The best *arroz* needs first-class ingredients, such as Valencia or Italian *arborio* rice, home-made stock and free-range chicken, added to a *sofrito* base of onions slowly cooked with tomato. This serves four, accompanied by a mixed salad and crusty bread.

400g/14oz free-range chicken
700ml/1¼ pints/2½ cups chicken stock (broth)
½ tsp saffron strands
1 large red pepper
4 tbs olive oil
1 large onion, peeled and chopped
2 ripe tomatoes, peeled and chopped
1 clove garlic, peeled and chopped
salt
freshly milled black pepper
1 green pepper, seeded and chopped
350g/12oz/1¼ cups short-grained rice
50g/2oz fresh shelled (or frozen) peas

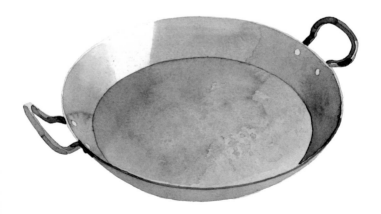

Cut the chicken into smallish serving pieces, taking care to leave some skin on to preserve moisture and succulence. Heat the stock without boiling, then set it aside. Put the saffron into a teacup, add a little hot stock and allow to infuse for at least 30 minutes.

Remove the cap and seeds of the red pepper and slice in half from top to bottom. Dice one half; slice the other into long, thin strips and put them to one side.

Heat the olive oil in a heavy 28cm/11 inch frying pan or, if you have one, a small *paella* pan. Fry the chicken pieces on all sides until golden. Remove and drain on kitchen paper (paper towel).

Add the onion, lower the heat and cook until soft and golden (about 5 minutes). Add the tomatoes and garlic, season and cook slowly, stirring occasionally for 8–10 minutes longer. Add the diced green and red peppers, cover and cook for 5 more minutes, stirring once or twice.

Add the rice and stir-fry for 2–3 minutes. Pour in all the stock, raise the heat to medium and cook until most of the liquid has evaporated (10–12 minutes), stirring frequently. Push in the chicken pieces, spaced evenly, then arrange the red pepper strips over the rice like the spokes of a wheel. Scatter over the peas, pour in the saffron liquid, cover tightly and cook gently for 15 minutes longer. The rice should now be tender and dry. Leave to rest uncovered for 3 minutes before serving. Scrape the bottom of the pan to ensure that each portion has a little of the rice crust – for many families, this is the most prized part of the dish!

WILD RICE

Wild rice adds an interesting taste and texture to regular long-grained rice, its dark grains contrasting dramatically with the white. This makes perfect, fluffy rice, ideal for serving with almost anything, but especially Indian and south-east Asian curries, Chinese, Korean and Japanese dishes. Makes enough for four.

40g/1½oz/2½ tbs wild rice
1 litre/1¾ pints/3½ cups water
350g/12oz/1½ cups long-grained rice

Put the wild rice and 450ml/³/₄ pint/1½ cups water in a small pot. Cover and bring to the boil, then reduce the heat and simmer for about 30 minutes. Drain. (May be done in advance.)

Wash the long-grained rice in plenty of fresh water, gently squeezing with your fingers to release some starch. Rinse repeatedly until the water is no longer cloudy, then drain. Put the wild rice and the washed long-grained rice into a pot with a tight-fitting lid, mixing well. Add the remaining water. Bring to the boil, cover tightly and reduce the heat to minimum. Cook for exactly 15 minutes; the rice should be tender and fluffy. Serve immediately.

FRAGRANT RICE WITH FRESH HERBS

Chopped aromatic herbs give fragrant long-grained rice a pleasant green speckled appearance, a delightful flavour and a sweet perfume. Use at least three of the following herbs: parsley, chives, mint, basil, chervil, tarragon, sorrel and coriander (cilantro). Serve as an accompaniment.

300g/11oz/1½ cups basmati or 'Thai fragrant' rice
560ml/1 pint/2 cups water
½ tsp salt
chopped fresh herbs to fill a teacup

Wash the rice in fresh water, gently squeezing the grains to remove some starch. Rinse several times and drain.

Put the rice into a pot. Add the water and salt. Bring to the boil, reduce the heat to minimum and cover tightly. Cook for 15 minutes. Remove the cover, gently mix in the fresh herbs and serve straight away.

COCONUT RICE

· · · · · · · · · ·

This exotic aromatic rice is exceptionally easy to make and goes very well with curries, stir-fried vegetables, and Indian *dals* and relishes. Unsweetened canned coconut milk from Thailand and other tropical countries is readily available; alternatively, you can use coconut milk powder and add hot water as directed on the packet instructions. Makes enough for four servings.

350g/12oz/1 ½ cups long-grained rice
400ml/14 fl oz/1 ½ cups coconut milk
½ tsp salt
1 curry leaf or 1 bay leaf
4 green or black cardamom pods
4 cloves
small piece of cinnamon

Wash the rice, squeezing the grains gently to release excess starch. Rinse several times and drain. Put the rice and the rest of the ingredients into a pot with a tight-fitting lid. Bring to the boil, reduce the heat to minimum, cover tightly and cook gently for 20 minutes. Remove the leaf and spices before serving.

KEDGEREE
· · · · · · · · · ·

At the turn of the century *kedgeree* was a favourite component of grand, old-fashioned British breakfasts. An Anglo-Indian dish, kedgeree derives from Hindi *khichri*, a traditional dish of rice, lentils, eggs and spices. Although salmon is often substituted, many prefer the mild-flavoured flaky flesh of fresh or smoked haddock. With its subtle spicing and attractive garnishes, this version makes a very pleasant light lunch or supper and is ample for four people.

Court bouillon
1 bay leaf
3 sprigs of parsley
1 carrot, scrubbed and chopped
$\frac{1}{2}$ stick (stalk) of celery
1 onion, peeled and quartered
700ml/1$\frac{1}{4}$ pints/2$\frac{1}{2}$ cups water
salt
freshly milled black pepper

350g/12oz filleted smoked or fresh haddock or salmon
2 cloves of garlic, peeled
1cm/$\frac{1}{2}$ inch piece of ginger, peeled
2 fresh chilies, washed and seeded
4 tbs sunflower or peanut oil
225g/8oz/1 cup long-grained rice,
washed and drained
2 tsp curry powder
$\frac{1}{2}$ tsp turmeric
2 tbs raisins

To garnish:
2 hard-boiled (hard-cooked) eggs, finely chopped
1 banana, peeled and chopped
40g/1$\frac{1}{2}$oz peanuts, crushed or chopped
1 lemon, quartered
handful of coriander (cilantro), washed and chopped

Put the bay leaf, parsley, carrot, celery and 2 onion quarters into a pan large enough to accommodate the fish. Add the water, season and bring to the boil. Cover, reduce the heat and simmer for 15 minutes. Add the fish, bring back to a simmer, cover the pan and poach for 6–8 minutes. Meanwhile, put the remaining onion quarters, garlic, ginger, chilies and 3 tbs oil into the bowl of a food processor. Reduce to a paste. When it has cooked, lift out the fish. Remove and discard the skin, flake the flesh and put it to one side, then strain and reserve the *court bouillon*.

Heat the remaining oil in a wide, heavy pan, add the paste and stir-fry for 1 minute. Add the rice, curry powder and turmeric and stir for 30 seconds. Add the strained *court bouillon*, bring to the boil, reduce the heat, cover and cook until the rice is dry and the grains are tender. Check the seasoning, then gently mix in the flaked fish and the raisins. Garnish with chopped eggs, bananas, peanuts and lemon quarters (or serve them separately in little bowls). Sprinkle coriander over the *kedgeree* and serve immediately.

NASI GORENG

· · · · · · · · · ·

There are many variations on this classic fried rice dish from Indonesia, for which the choice of garnishes is almost as important as the rice base. Try any of these combinations: finely diced tomatoes, radishes and cucumber; finely shredded raw lettuce or Chinese leaf cabbage; finely sliced spring onions (scallions); chopped bananas; fried, thinly sliced onion or shallots; finely chopped fried ham or bacon; thin strips of omelette or chopped hard-boiled (hard-cooked) eggs; or chopped nuts. Alternatively, cooked shrimps or other seafood may be substituted. Serves six people as a rice accompaniment or four as a light meal.

400g/15oz/2 cups long-grained rice
560ml/1 pint/2 cups water
3 tbs peanut oil
1 red onion or 4 shallots, peeled and chopped
1 clove of garlic, peeled and chopped
2 fresh chilies, washed, seeded and chopped
2 peeled tomatoes (fresh or canned), finely chopped
110g/4oz sliced mushrooms (optional)
small green pepper, cored, seeded and diced (optional)
1 1/2 tbs light soy sauce
1/2–1 tsp bottled chili sauce (optional)

Wash the rice, squeezing the grains gently to release some starch. Rinse several times and drain. Put the rice and 560ml/1 pint/2 cups fresh water into a pot with a tight-fitting lid. Bring to the boil, then cover, reduce the heat and simmer as gently as possible for 12 minutes. Remove the cover and set aside for several hours, to cool.

Heat the oil in a wok or in a wide, heavy pan. Stir-fry the onion or shallots, garlic and chilies for 2 minutes, then add the tomatoes, and the mushrooms and pepper (if desired). Stir-fry for 3 minutes longer. Add the cooked rice, break up any lumps and stir-fry over a moderately low heat for about 6 minutes. Add the soy sauce (and the chili sauce if using), and stir-fry for another minute. Serve immediately with at least 3 of the garnishes suggested above; these can be scattered over the rice or served separately in little bowls.

BULGUR PILAF
· · · · · · · · · ·

Cracked wheat makes an excellent *pilaf* which goes very well with stews and grilled (broiled) meat or poultry. For vegetarians, the pilaf, tomato salad and garlicky yoghurt combine to make a delicious balanced meal, serving four.

3 tbs olive oil
1 small onion, peeled and finely chopped
$1/2$ tsp ground cumin
$1/2$ tsp ground coriander
225g/8oz/1 cup *bulgur* (cracked wheat)
salt
560ml/1 pint/2 cups chicken or vegetable stock (broth)
handful of fresh parsley, washed and chopped

Heat the oil in a pan with a tight-fitting lid. Sauté the onion until soft. Add the spices, mix well and cook gently for 1 minute longer. Add the *bulgur* and sauté for 3 minutes. Season, add the stock and stir while the liquid comes to the boil. Cover tightly, reduce the heat to minimum and cook for about 20 minutes. The *pilaf* should be dry and tender. Gently mix in the parsley and serve.

Tomato salad
350g/12oz tomatoes, washed and sliced
225g/8oz cucumber, washed, peeled and sliced
4 spring onions (scallions), chopped
handful of fresh mint, washed and chopped
salt
freshly milled black pepper
3 tbs extra virgin olive oil
juice of half a lemon

Arrange the sliced tomato and cucumber on a plate in concentric overlapping rings. Scatter the spring onions and mint over them, and season. Beat the olive oil and lemon juice with a teaspoon, pour over the salad and serve immediately.

Garlicky yoghurt
200g/7oz/²⁄₃ cup strained yoghurt
1 clove of garlic
2 tbs pine nuts
pinch of salt
freshly milled black pepper
pinch of cayenne
1 tbs olive oil

Beat the yoghurt until creamy. Put it in a bowl. With
a mortar and pestle, pound to a paste the garlic, pine
nuts, salt, pepper, cayenne and olive oil. Stir the
paste into the yoghurt. Cover and set aside for 30–60
minutes to allow the flavours to develop; the yoghurt
may also be served straight away.

Couscous with Tagine
. . . .

Traditionally, *couscous* is steamed in double steamer called a *couscousier;* meat or vegetables stew in the lower chamber and the rising steam cooks the pasta in the upper chamber. In the following simplified recipe, the *couscous* is soaked in water to swell the grains, then heated in the oven or on top of the stove. Served with a *tagine* or stew and a little *harissa,* this makes a complete meal for four people.

Harissa

This fiery paste is usually diluted and served separately in a bowl. This makes 6–8 tbs of *harissa,* which, stored in a sealed and refrigerated jar, will keep well for several weeks. The heat of the chilies varies according to the varieties used; as a rule of thumb, the smaller the pepper, the hotter it will be, so it is up to the individual to adjust the quantities accordingly.

> 75g/3oz dried chilies
> 2 tsp caraway seeds
> 2 tsp cumin seeds
> 2 tsp coriander seeds
> 4 cloves of garlic, peeled and sliced
> 2 tsp dried mint
> 2 tsp paprika
> 1 tsp salt
> 4 tbs olive oil

Crush the chilies – this can be done in a food processor, clean coffee grinder or with a mortar and pestle. Grind the caraway, cumin and coriander seeds. In a food processor, combine the chilies and ground spices with the garlic, mint, paprika, salt and 2 tbs of olive oil, and blend to a coarse paste. Spoon the *harissa* into a clean jar, cover with the remaining oil, seal and keep refrigerated until required.

Couscous and tagine
350g/12oz/2 cups *couscous*
1¼ litres/2 pints/4 cups water
110ml/4fl oz/½ cup olive oil
1 chicken, cut into small serving pieces
1 large onion, peeled and chopped
450g/1lb cooked chick peas (canned ones are fine)
2 carrots, scrubbed and chopped
2 sweet peppers, washed, seeded and chopped
350g/12oz peeled and chopped tomatoes (fresh or canned)
1 tbs tomato purée (paste)
1 tbs paprika
1–2 tsp cayenne
salt
175g/6oz courgettes (zucchini), washed and diced
110g/4oz chopped dates
25g/1oz raisins
handful of fresh coriander (cilantro), washed and chopped

Put the *couscous* in a bowl. Add half the water, turning the grains with your fingers to separate any lumps. Mix a few times while they swell.

Meanwhile, heat 4 tbs of olive oil in a casserole. Fry the chicken pieces until evenly golden-brown, then remove and reserve them. Add the onion and fry until soft and golden. Put in the chick peas, carrots, sweet peppers, tomatoes and tomato purée, paprika, cayenne (to taste), and season. Return the chicken to the casserole, add the rest of the water, mix well and cover tightly. Reduce the heat to minimum and simmer for 35–40 minutes.

About 15 minutes before the stew is ready, add the courgettes, dates and raisins to the *tagine*. Put the swollen *couscous* and 4 tbs of olive oil into a pan. Mix well. Cover the pan and heat in a moderate oven or on top of the stove. Garnish the *tagine* with coriander, and serve with the couscous and a little bowl of *harissa*, diluted with a few spoonfuls of the *tagine* juices.